no /ex 11/3/12

SUPER SPORTS STAR

PEYTON MANNING

Ken Rappoport

Enslow Publishers, Inc.

40 Industrial Road   PO Box 38
Box 398   Aldershot
Berkeley Heights, NJ 07922   Hants GU12 6BP
USA   UK

http://www.enslow.com

Library of Congress Cataloging-in-Publication Data

Rappoport, Ken.
    Super sports star Peyton Manning / Ken Rappoport.
        p. cm. — (Super sports star)
    Summary: Discusses the personal life and football career of Indianapolis Colts quarterback Peyton Manning.
    Includes bibliographical references and index.
    ISBN 0-7660-2079-7
    1. Manning, Peyton—Juvenile literature. 2. Football players—United States—Biography—Juvenile literature. [1. Manning, Peyton. 2. Football players.] I. Title. II. Series.
    GV939.M289 R37   2003
    796.332'092—dc21

                                                                    2002012334

Printed in the United States of America

10 9 8 7 6 5 4 3 2 1

To Our Readers:
We have done our best to make sure all Internet Addresses in this book were active and appropriate when we went to press. However, the author and the publisher have no control over and assume no liability for the material available on those Internet sites or on other Web sites they may link to. Any comments or suggestions can be sent by e-mail to comments@enslow.com or to the address on the back cover.

Photo Credits: © Vernon Biever/NFL photos, p. 6; © Scott Boehm/NFL Photos, pp. 9, 12, 18; © Tom Croke/NFL Photos, p. 35; © David Drapkin/NFL Photos, p. 42; © Paul Jasienski/NFL Photos, p. 10; © Allen Kee/NFL Photos, pp. 20, 26, 28, 30, 32; © Don Larson/NFL Photos, p. 4; © Marty Morrow/NFL Photos, pp. 1, 17; © Al Pereira/NFL Photos, pp. 24, 34, 38; © James D. Smith/NFL Photos, pp. 13, 23, 40; © Jim Turner/NFL Photos, p. 16; © Ed Webber/NFL Photos, p. 45.

Cover Photo: © Marty Morrow/NFL Photos.

CONTENTS

Introduction

Peyton Manning could just be the perfect quarterback. He is six feet five inches tall and weighs 230 pounds. He is tall, strong, and is quick on his feet. Manning also throws the football quickly. That makes him hard to tackle.

Manning learned to love the game when he was a kid. His father, Archie Manning, was also a star quarterback. Peyton learned from his dad what it takes to be a leader. Peyton never stops practicing. He is always working hard to make himself better.

No wonder Manning has become one of the National Football League's top quarterbacks faster than anyone expected.

CHAPTER 1

Dunking the Dolphins

It was late in the 1999 NFL season. Indianapolis Colts quarterback Peyton Manning looked over the defense. Then he bent over center.

It was first and ten on the Colts' 32-yard line. They had 68 yards to go for a score. The game with the Miami Dolphins was tied, 34–34. But there were only thirty-one seconds left. Could Manning help break the tie?

It was a tough spot for Manning. Earlier in the season, he faced the same Dolphin team. During that game, the clock was running out, as it was now. Then, he had thrown a long pass. It was intercepted and the Colts lost.

Manning had watched that replay many times. He promised himself he would not make the same mistake again. This time, he would be more careful.

Manning took the snap from center. He dropped back. He completed a 16-yard pass over the middle. Time out. Now the Colts were on their own 48-yard line with only twenty-four seconds to go.

Manning tossed another short pass up the middle. The Colts gained another 18 yards. They were on the Dolphins' 34-yard line. The Colts called another time-out.

Now Manning sent star running back Edgerrin James into the line. Another eleven seconds ticked off the clock. It was time for the Colts' field goal kicker. If he could kick the ball through the goal posts, it would give the Colts a three-point lead.

The teams lined up with twelve seconds left. The ball was snapped back and placed on the ground for the kick. The kick sailed right through the goal posts. The Colts won, 37–34.

A newcomer had done better than one of the game's best quarterbacks, Dolphins great Dan Marino.

Peyton Manning throws downfield.

"Peyton's the new sheriff in town," said Colts tight end Ken Dilger. "I think he kind of proved today that he's the heir to Dan Marino."

Manning was only in his second year in the NFL. He was not thinking about Marino. But Manning did show he was a quick learner. And that he was one of the NFL's top young quarterbacks. Manning had come a long way in a short time.

Manning looks for an open receiver.

Born to Be a Quarterback

Imagine if you could see an NFL game from the sidelines. You could go into the locker room after the game. You could talk to your favorite stars. You could be on the field playing catch. Not in your backyard, but in an actual NFL stadium. Growing up, Peyton Manning was able to do just that.

Manning's father was a quarterback. Archie Manning was named a college All-American at the University of Mississippi. He was an all-star with the New Orleans Saints.

Being the son of Archie Manning had its rewards. Sundays were spent in the New Orleans Superdome watching his father play. When the game was over, the fans went home. Peyton did not go home. He went to the locker room with his older brother, Cooper. They ate candy bars and made footballs out of tape. Out on the NFL field, they played football. Peyton wanted to be a football star just like his dad.

Peyton Manning was born on March 24, 1976. He grew up in the city of New Orleans in Louisiana. In a big yellow house, he would lie awake at night and listen to tapes of old radio broadcasts of his father's games. Peyton enjoyed hearing stories about his father's college days.

As a kid, Peyton Manning enjoyed listening to old tapes of his father's games.

He loved football. His older brother, Cooper, and younger brother, Eli, loved the sport, too.

In the eighth grade, Peyton started thinking about a football career. "I started working at the (quarterback) position a little bit," Peyton said. "I'd ask questions of my dad and my teammates." Peyton was a hard worker. He spent a lot of his time studying his father's game films. He knew more about football than almost anyone his age.

Peyton was only in his second year of high school when he was the starting quarterback. He played for Isidore Newman, a small private school. And guess who was

Peyton Manning wanted to be a football star from the time he was a kid.

Peyton's favorite receiver? His brother Cooper. Cooper was the school's star pass catcher.

Peyton had an amazing high school career. He passed for more than 7,000 yards. He had ninety-two touchdown passes. He led his school to thirty-four wins. He only lost five games in three seasons. Stories about Peyton were in national sports magazines and newspapers. He was also on television.

★★★ **UP CLOSE**

Peyton Manning holds 42 NCAA, SEC, and Tennessee records.

All the nation's top college football teams wanted Peyton to play for them. Which school would Peyton Manning choose?

Bowling Them Over

It was college decision day. In a room filled with reporters and television cameras, Peyton Manning stepped to the microphone. Then he surprised the sports world.

It had been a tough choice for Manning. His father had starred at the University of Mississippi. His brother Cooper had played there before an injury ended his career. Manning was expected to go there, too. Instead, he chose the University of Tennessee. He thought he had a better chance of winning there.

"I wanted to follow my heart," Manning said at the 1994 news conference. "But instead I followed my mind."

The decision created a lot of bad feelings. He received letters from angry Mississippi fans.

Manning thought he was going to spend his

first year watching from the sidelines. In the season's fourth game against Mississippi State, the Tennessee Volunteers' quarterback was hurt. The back-up quarterback was also injured. Now Manning had to carry the team. He had to become a leader. It was scary: He was only a freshman in his first month of college football.

The game was tied, 7–7, just before halftime. The ball was on the Tennessee 22-yard line. It was a long way—78 yards—to the goal line. Play after play Manning moved the Volunteers down

Peyton Manning chose to play college football at the University of Tennessee.

the field. The Volunteers were inside the 20 when Manning found a receiver open. He fired a pass. Touchdown! The Volunteers soon led, 14–7.

Even though the Volunteers lost that game, Manning showed he was a leader.

Peyton Manning was back in the lineup the following week. Now the Volunteers started winning. With Manning as a starter, they won six of seven games. He had helped turn a losing team into a winning one.

"Peyton's becoming a very confident quarterback," said guard Kevin Mayes. "There's a different look in his eye now when he steps into a huddle."

Peyton Manning gets ready to throw another touchdown pass.

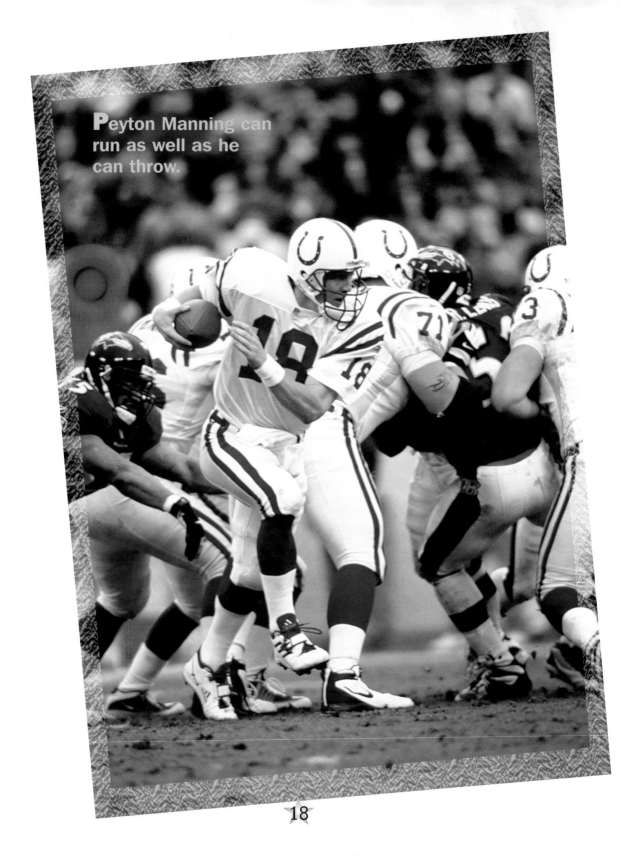

Peyton Manning can run as well as he can throw.

It was hard to believe that Manning, only in his first year in college, was leading his team to the Gator Bowl. Peyton Manning and the Volunteers went up against the Virginia Tech Hokies in a bowl game.

Early in the game, the Volunteers found themselves a long way from the goal line. Manning looked over the defense. The Hokies were playing back. They expected Manning to pass. He fooled them and ran for 32 yards. "They gave me the opportunity to run and I just wanted to show people I could run a little bit," Manning said.

Manning had shown the Hokies that he could run. Then he showed them he could throw. He threw a 36-yard touchdown pass. Tennessee won, 45–23.

Although Peyton Manning was younger than most of the players on the field, he had lifted his team to great heights. He was confident. He was growing up quickly in the fast-paced world of big-time college football.

Glory Days

During his second year at Tennessee, all eyes were on Peyton Manning. It was a week after one of the worst losses in Tennessee's football history.

All week he had been thinking about the 62–37 loss to the University of Florida. Now he had to think about Mississippi State. The Bulldogs were a tough team. Manning had lost to them as a freshman the year before.

It was the fourth game of the 1995 season. A noisy crowd of 95,232 filled Tennessee's Neyland Stadium. The fans were waiting to see what Manning could do. After one quarter, they had not seen much. The Volunteers could only manage two field goals for a 6–0 lead.

In the second quarter, the Volunteers were on their own 34-yard line. It was third down and six yards to go for a first down. If they did not make the first down, they would be forced to punt. The offensive team needs to gain ten yards on four chances, known as downs. Otherwise, it has to give the ball back to the other team.

Manning set the offense into motion. He rolled to his left. He faked a pass and raced eight yards for the first down.

Manning then completed a 40-yard pass. The Volunteers were now on the Mississippi State 7-yard line. They scored a touchdown on a running play.

Then Tennessee had a choice. Should they kick the ball through the goal posts for one point? Or run a play into the end zone for two points? They decided to run the play. Manning completed a pass for a 2-point conversion. His team led, 14–0. The landslide had begun. The Volunteers won, 52–14.

Peyton Manning was winning again. But there was another test ahead. This time, it was against

★★ UP CLOSE
★

Since turning pro in 1998, Manning started every game for the Colts for five straight seasons—a team record.

Peyton Manning waits for a receiver to get open downfield.

the Alabama Crimson Tide. The Volunteers had not beaten the Crimson Tide in nine seasons. "There was a lot of unhappiness in Tennessee [about the winless streak]," Manning said.

On the very first play of the game, Manning threw an 80-yard touchdown pass. He passed for 301 yards and finished with three touchdown passes. The Volunteers won, 41–14.

The loss to Florida was now a distant memory. Manning led his team to win nine games in a row. The Volunteers capped the season

Peyton Manning had the option of graduating from college one year early.

24

with a 20–14 win over Ohio State in the Citrus Bowl. It was an amazing year for Peyton Manning. He set a college record when only four of his 380 passes were intercepted.

The following season, Manning led the Volunteers back to the Citrus Bowl. This time, they beat Northwestern, 48–28. Manning was also working hard in the classroom. After three years, he had enough credits to graduate with honors. He could leave school one year early to join the NFL.

The fans knew they could lose Peyton. During the Northwestern game they chanted, "Stay, Peyton, stay!"

Manning had to decide if he would stay in Tennessee or turn pro.

Making More Memories

Thank You, Peyton.

A big orange billboard said it all.

Peyton Manning had made his decision. He would stay in school for his senior year. The students threw parties all over campus.

His decision surprised some people. Many star athletes leave school early to go to the pros. They want to move on. But college football was too much fun for Manning. He did not want to give it up just yet. As he said, "I came back to create more memories."

Manning told the world of his decision in the winter of 1997.

"When Peyton made his announcement," said Volunteers coach Phillip Fullmer, "I heard the earth shake."

Manning wanted to make his final year in college a special one. And he did. He led the

When Peyton Manning played for the University of Tennessee, he passed for 523 yards in one game.

Volunteers to win after win. The Volunteers met the University of Kentucky in a late season game. Both teams were having good seasons.

Manning's play had caught the attention of the nation. And Tim Couch, Kentucky's star quarterback, also had a strong arm. So, everyone expected the sky to be filled with footballs. They were not disappointed.

Couch's 476 passing yards set a Kentucky record. Manning did better. He passed for 523 yards and five touchdowns. It was a Volunteers' record for passing yardage. The Volunteers finished on top in a wild game, 59–31.

The next game was against the University of Auburn. If the Volunteers could beat them, they would win the Southeastern Conference (SEC) title. Early in the game, Manning threw a 40-yard touchdown pass. But the Vols were behind in the fourth quarter. Manning came to the rescue. He completed a 73-yard touchdown pass. Victory belonged to Tennessee, 30–29.

Peyton Manning
was chosen by the
Indianapolis Colts
as the number one
draft pick.

"SEC champs!" a beaming Manning said. "Sounds good, doesn't it?"

Then Manning was disappointed. The Volunteers lost to the University of Nebraska in the Orange Bowl. But he was happy with his college career. He had broken thirty-three school records. He also broke several national records. He led the Volunteers to an outstanding 39–6 record as a starter.

Manning had been number one in the hearts of fans. Then he was number one in the NFL draft. The Indianapolis Colts made Peyton Manning the top pick. Manning was proud of the honor. But he knew he still had to prove himself as a pro. "I'm looking forward to the challenge," he said.

CHAPTER
6

A Frisky Colt

Peyton Manning was struggling. After four games in the pros, he was still looking for his first victory.

Coming up was a game with the San Diego Chargers. But it was more than just another game. It matched two of the NFL's promising young quarterbacks. Who was better, Peyton Manning of the Colts or Ryan Leaf of the Chargers?

The year before, they were considered the top two college quarterbacks in the country. They had never met on a football field, but they were always being compared to each other. At the 1998 NFL draft, Manning was chosen No. 1 and Leaf was No. 2. And now they were about to clash.

The Colts took an early lead. They intercepted a pass by Leaf. Manning quickly had the Colts in the end zone with a 19-yard pass.

Peyton Manning beat Ryan Leaf and the Chargers for his first NFL win.

Late in the game, the Colts held a 14–6 lead. Leaf brought the Chargers to life. He completed a 56-yard pass play. Then a running touchdown by the Chargers cut the Colts' lead to 14–12. But the Chargers would get no closer. The Colts added a field goal. They held on to win, 17–12. The victory was special to Manning. "You're always going to remember your first one," he said after the game.

The Colts won only two more games in Manning's rookie year. They finished with a 3–13 record for the second straight year. In one season with the Colts, Peyton Manning had lost

Peyton Manning waits to make the perfect pass.

two more games than in his eight years of high school and college ball combined.

But there was also some good news. Manning had put together the best rookie season in NFL history. He was the only NFL quarterback to have taken every snap for his team in 1998. With twenty-six touchdown passes, he broke Charlie Conerly's rookie record. That was a big deal in the Manning household, because Conerly was an all-star quarterback at Mississippi and the New York Giants in the NFL. The Mannings all loved him. "I'm not a big individual records guy," Manning said, "but that's kind of special."

Records were great, all right. Now all Peyton Manning had to do was learn how to win in the big leagues.

★
★★
★ **UP CLOSE**

In January 1999, Peyton Manning was named one of ten outstanding young Americans by the United States Junior Chamber of Commerce.

The Manning Touch

Look out NFL, here come the Colts. Faster than you could say Peyton Manning, the Colts were suddenly battling for the division title. It did not seem possible to go from last to first in one season. But Manning and his teammates were doing their best to make it happen.

It was only Manning's second year in the NFL. Yet he was the best known player on his team. The Colts had one of the NFL's top offenses in 1999. The Colts' defense was also strong.

Manning's football work habits had not changed since he was eleven years old. "He's always working on something," said Colts defensive end Mark Thomas. "He's here [practice field] early and stays late."

Peyton Manning practices on
his own and with his team.

When Manning's practice was over, he did extra work on his own. He joined the special teams practice. He ran up and down the field on kickoff coverage. And then he did more passing practice. Finally, he studied videotapes and the playbook.

Early in the 1999 season, Manning faced one of his toughest tests. He was going against the San Diego Chargers, one of the NFL's top defensive teams.

With the game in the fourth quarter, the Colts trailed, 19–13. To win, they had to score a touchdown. But the goal line was 83 yards away. Manning quickly moved the Colts down the field. Eight plays later, they were in the end zone. Manning ran 12 yards for the touchdown. To top it off, he later threw a 26-yard touchdown pass. The Colts won, 27–19. What a day for Manning. Passing for 404 yards, he broke the Colts' team record held by Johnny Unitas.

Victories were piling up. The Colts were

Peyton Manning broke the Colts record for passing yards in a game when he threw for 404 yards against the San Diego Chargers.

within range of the division title. The Washington Redskins were next. The Colts needed one more win to go for the championship. They were behind, 13–10, going into the fourth quarter. Manning threw a short touchdown pass to give the Colts the lead. They later added a rushing touchdown to beat the Redskins, 24–21. They did it. They had completely reversed their 1998, 3–13 record, with 13–3 in 1999. The Colts were going to the playoffs. It was the greatest turnaround in NFL history.

Suddenly, the Colts had become one of the NFL's top teams.

During the 2000 season, Manning set a new Colts' record with thirty-three touchdown passes in one season. The Colts finished with a 10–6 record and made the playoffs for the second year in a row.

Manning was again at the top of his game in 2001. The Colts were not and missed the playoffs. But in 2002 they were back! Manning was better than ever. He set an important league record. He became the only player in NFL history with 4,000 or more passing yards in four straight years. For the third time in five years, Manning was named to the Pro Bowl. That is the NFL's all-star game.

Off the field, Manning was also making news. He started a charity called the PeyBack Foundation. It raises money for children in need. One example was a series of high school football games called the "PeyBack Classic." The games were played in the Colts' own

Peyton Manning led the Colts into the playoffs in 1999, 2000, and 2002.

stadium. They raised $50,000 for the athletic programs of five high schools in Indianapolis.

Manning also found time in the off-season to go back to school. He worked towards a master's degree in sports management at Tennessee.

Peyton Manning is married. His wife Ashley is from Memphis, Tennessee and went to the University of Virginia.

In just a few short years, Peyton Manning had become a big star. Manning received a rare honor when his jersey was retired at Tennessee. He was following in his father's footsteps. In high school, Manning was known as Archie Manning's son. But he worked hard to become a big name in his own right. Now he is one of the best quarterbacks in the NFL.

CAREER STATISTICS

NFL									
Passing									
Year	Team	GP	Comp.	Att.	Yds.	Pct.	TDs	Int.	Rating
1998	Indianapolis	16	326	575	3,739	56.7	26	28	71.2
1999	Indianapolis	16	331	533	4,135	62.1	26	15	90.7
2000	Indianapolis	16	357	571	4,413	62.5	33	15	94.7
2001	Indianapolis	16	343	547	4,131	62.7	26	23	84.1
2002	Indianapolis	16	392	591	4,200	66.3	27	19	88.8
Totals		80	1,749	2,817	20,618	62.1	138	100	85.9

Rushing						
Year	Team	GP	Att.	Yds.	Avg.	TDs
1998	Indianapolis	16	15	62	4.1	0
1999	Indianapolis	16	35	73	2.1	2
2000	Indianapolis	16	37	116	3.1	1
2001	Indianapolis	16	35	157	4.5	4
2002	Indianapolis	16	38	148	3.9	2
Totals		80	160	556	3.5	9

GP–Games Played
GS–Games Started
Att.–Passes Attempted
Comp.–Passes Completed

Pct.–Percentage of Passes Completed
Yds.–Yards Passing
TD–Touchdown Passes

Int.–Interceptions
No.–Number of carries

44

Where to Write to Peyton Manning

Mr. Peyton Manning
c/o The Indianapolis Colts
7001 West 56th Street
Indianapolis, IN 46254

Peyton Manning has made a name for himself as one of the NFL's best quarterbacks.

WORDS TO KNOW

draft—A selection of players by teams, who take turns choosing the players they want.

freshman—A ninth-grade student in high school or a first-year student in college.

quarterback—He is in charge of the offense. He calls the plays, sometimes with help from the bench. The quarterback can either pass the ball, hand it off to a running back, or keep it and run.

rookie—A player in his first full season in professional sports.

senior—A twelfth-grade student in high school or a fourth-year student in college.

tight end—Usually a big player who catches passes and blocks for runners.

READING ABOUT

Books

Buckley, James. *Peyton Manning: Born to Play.* New York: Dorling Kindersley Publishing Co., 2001.

Frisaro, Joe. *Peyton Manning: Passing Legacy.* Chicago: Sports Publishing, Inc., 1999.

Hopping, Lorraine Jean and Christopher Egan. *Sports Hall of Fame.* New York: Mondo Publishing, 2001.

Savage, Jeff. *Peyton Manning: Precision Passer.* Minneapolis, Minn.: Lerner Publications, 2001.

Internet Addresses

The Official Web Site of the Indianapolis Colts
<http://www.colts.com/>

Official Peyton Manning Web Site
<http://www.peytonmanning.com>

INDEX